HUMAN TETRIS

ELEVEN
11:11
ELEVEN
PRESS

VI KHI NAO & ALI RAZ

Vi Khi Nao Ar

HUMAN TETRIS
Copyright © 2019 by Vi Khi Nao & Ali Raz
All rights reserved.
This book may not be reproduced in whole or in part, except for the inclusion of brief quotations in a review, without permission in writing from the author or publisher. No part of this publication may be reproduced, stored in or introduced into a retrieval system, or transmitted, in any form, or by any means (electronic, mechanical, photocopying, recording, or otherwise), without prior permission of the publisher. Requests for permission should be directed to 1111@1111press.com, or mailed to 11:11 Press LLC, 4757 15th Ave S., Minneapolis, MN 55407

Cover & Layout by Vi Khi Nao & Ali Raz
Design & Formatting by Ashley Bernhardt & J.N. Habiger

LCCN: 2019938355
978-1-948687-08-9 (paperback)
978-1-948687-09-6 (ebook)

FIRST AMERICAN EDITION

Printed in the United States of America
9 8 7 6 5 4 3 2 1

CONTENTS

1	close-minded socialist iso cool cucumber
2	show me the conspiracy
3	spatchcock me silly
4	mutated gene seeks similar
5	fornication isn't my thing
6	iso extraordinary cause and effect
7	love in the post-era of the cholera
8	not my self to night
9	pseudo-weirdo leo 4 opposite
10	ken looking for his ryu
11	ophthalmologist iso love-scam artist
12	playtest
13	be my beehive, be my boner & clyde
14	cute boi looking for a bot
15	fat bumblebee in search of her honey
16	looking for my panadol
17	let me use your body to weaponize lust
18	a love affair for the ages
19	human cow in search of her human wind-
20	r u the one for me?
21	polar femme 4 solar femme
22	looking for my happy ending
23	myopic cinderella 4 non-binary cinder
24	inun-date me with chocolate
25	help me tongue-choreograph our desire
26	need a furry for the winter
27	seeking an abrasion-resistant lover
28	a date for the movies
29	be my telescopic cancer survivor
30	netflix and chill

NOT CONSENT

#	
31	take elevator e to the penthouse of my heart
32	i wanna know what love is
33	intersectional sofa lesbians only!
34	looking for my final girl
35	your appetizer for my dessert
36	be my extremity
37	invasion is a kind of psychic sedation
38	be my boyrfriend
39	wear a dress & help this
40	a touch of sin
41	amnesia inside a sapphic breeze?
42	tarzan seeks jane
43	queen of queer sublet
44	pedantic but not pediatric
45	my new year resolutions
46	will mow your lawn for free
47	dyslexic sex to replace exquisite love
48	i want to fall in love again
49	x-ray my nonbinary body w/ with your binary eyes
50	partner wanted for one date
51	jovial about casual strangulation?
52	not on the rebound
53	kiss me a million times already
54	chill boi iso fwb
55	zero tolerance for academic femme
56	iso nerdy slut
57	goat shepherd iso cookie warmer femme or cutter
58	a date for the new year
59	ex-genderfluid subaru wants a sono sion w/ conservative breasts
60	love me like iced coffee

Advance Praise for Human Tetris

These poems are clever meals, feeding us the jumpy truth about our inner longings. Devilish reminders that love is often just a combination of peculiar proclivities—reassurances that desire is always particular and unflinchingly weird.

    Raluca Albu, Bomb Magazine

Me: Middle-aged writer, mind-softened by early summer heat, weary of humankind. *You:* Tender word orgy, prickly song, mesmerizing game, thrilling voice of multiples.

    Nathaniel Popkin, Cleaver Magazine

In Vi Khi Nao & Ali Raz vertically-integrated collaborative text, all subjectivity is a game of *Human Tetris*.

    Louis Armand, *Director of the Centre for Critical & Cultural Theory,* Charles University, Prague

What is *Human Tetris* by Vi Khi Nao and Ali Raz? A series of poems starring supreme anti-beings? Ultra-compressed and data-moshed versions of a(n) supposed ancient-Future? A sideways ethnographics of 21st century computer-simulated un-realities? Or, is it simply a self-eating parasite that could only exist in a digital Vantablack-tinged Dark Ages of the soon-to-be artifact'd meta-apocalypse? Maybe it is all of the above? Just know, with this text, Nao and Raz have perfectly encapsulated what it means, on the Kardashev scale, to (still) be a Type 0 Civilisation. Please shelve under: forward-thinking, outré, books where the Internet is pro(?)/antagonist and absolutely (like, I'm-still-fucking-shook) terrifying.

    Mike Kleine, Author of *Kanley Stubrick* and *Lonely Men Club*

Flirting with the absurdity of dating through digital devices culled from analogue word counts of print personals, *Human Tetris* catalogues kinks into an abundance so normal that poetry wins as ultimate release valve.

    Ariel Goldberg, Author of *The Estrangement Principle*

Me: wondering how two people can connect over off-kilter internet banter.
Human Tetris: Proving anything can happen if you just click send.

You might have to turn it, but this piece will fit in your life.

    Chris Margolin, The Poetry Question

Human Tetris is as complex as anything either writer has accomplished and impossibly more so for their successful layering here. It's a wild book, a fun book, and an informative book on the state of our blurred selves in the modern world.

    Grant Maierhofer, Author of *Peripatet* and *Drain Songs*

Human Tetris is a building lattice of interlocking online identities, exposing themselves at all times yet still coming off as detached by sheer geography, sheer facelessness, sheer screen-name anonymity. Like the curated spaces we lurk on the internet, it is as tongue-in-cheek as it is terrifyingly sincere, and you won't be able to look away. Get ready for a new scale of globalized game impossible to sit right in. This book doesn't offer playing rules, but little breadcrumbs to a final triumph forever out of reach--like a photo log of a star long dead, or a defunct message board about a movie that never reached release. All our forgotten diaries are still out there. *Human Tetris* imagines them stacking all the way up and filling the future with want.

    Dylan Krieger, Author of *Giving Godhead* and *The Mother Wart*

"Love is a transaction and I'm applying for a job. I'm applying to / your opening." These poems are an earnest reminder of how extravagantly weird any honest self-portrait should be / weirder still when the ideal audience of that self-portrait is meant to be a fantasy / a soul-mate / or simply an opportunity crackling flashing the other end / of the dating app / of the text. What is it to be seen / to be viewed / devoured / loved? What a peep into the center of the flower / what a delight.

    Carrie Lorig, Author of *The Pulp vs. The Throne*

Human Tetris

CLOSE-MINDED SOCIALIST ISO COOL CUCUMBER

Me: petite, myopic, smells fishy, tends to crush my lovers (in bed) from sheer weight & will, & I urinate (at least) twice a day

You: over 30, Asian, sexy, delusional, super yellow (from being too Asian) & heliotropic like a sunflower from smiling too much from loving me too much (of course)

@fuckmelikeafullmoon

Des Moines, IA near a post-Brexit thing called England

SHOW ME THE CONSPIRACY

Taco-loving sleep addict seeks a like-minded lizard. Let's cuddle and eat the whole winter through. Other activities, if absolutely necessary, may include: clipping newspapers, listening to Radiohead, and/or sniffing glue.

@delusionisright
Los Angeles, CA

SPATCHCOCK ME SILLY

Me: bi & organic (100% Chinese + a few % Egyptian), nori seaweed, salty, & I squirt decently like the fountain at Bellagio. Must eat/love durian, consider it as the most & only important status symbol.

You: English like fresh strawberry, charred by baby gem, pickled by bitter love, hairy in the right places @indecentlymadeinchina

Portland, ME

MUTATED GENE SEEKS SIMILAR

A yearning machine, ball of desire, seeks girl in red dress. Do you like to watch obscure films that disappear when you have watched them? Do you, too, pick your nose? Do you then lick the finger that picked it? I have spent too much time staring at a mirror, at the photo taped to the top-right corner of the mirror. If this sounds like you, hmu. @melons&rmezcal

Mexico City, Mexico

FORNICATION ISN'T MY THING

Eating is.
No way am I a sub. Though occasionally
I eat a 6 inch at subway, 6 inch being my dom. Just to remind
me that binary culture
is still food. ISO women who are bad carbohydrates, carbonated lemonade, sybarites
who don't switch or snitch.
Be my half-glazed donut.
Be my broken chicken wings dipped in copycat Chick-Fil-A Sauce.
Be my fat wife who has no place to hide.

@helplickmyfingershereandthere
Marfa, TX

ISO EXTRAORDINARY CAUSE AND EFFECT

ME: bad, dangerous, or crazy.
YOU: an open sore on my arm.
@fetishobject
Providence, RI

LOVE IN THE POST-ERA OF THE CHOLERA

A very low-battery Android S10 (aka androgynous, non-endearing Leo moon), ISO human electricity that can recharge me quickly. Don't be an electrical blackout when you plug me into you. Don't be the romantic fool that won't let me buy you dinners. Drink coffee excessively: 10 cups a day? That is me. Be my opposite: your cup size is Tea. Hit me up @notathreesomebombsell

Montreal, Canada

NOT MY SELF TO NIGHT

Be my cuddlebuddy. It is raining tonight.
I am out of bread, milk, and eggs. Shall we go shopping for me?

Me: Pit-stains on all my shirts, chocolate chip on my shoulder.

You: Exquisitely sexy and always on time.

@schmoozebutton

New York, NY

PSEUDO-WEIRDO LEO 4 OPPOSITE

Muslim progressive femme
who does not drink but believes in hand & purseholding.
Quiet bitches, hmm, beaches are sexy. Likes watching lovers eat bacon, cannot touch. Filmmaker by day,
bartender by night.
You: Jewish, of course, cozy & crazy,
You: cherubic, under 40, use dental floss every other day.
You: nomadic, Aquarius, hate cats & vegans, but are friendly to tofu that looks like pork.

Ambush me @lesbianmama

Lubbock, TX

KEN LOOKING FOR HIS RYU

Tired of another night of slicking around the mean streets alone—be the gin to my tonic, Vega's Chun-Li, other implicit combos. Yes: be implicit for me.

Interests: sauerkraut, torpedo sex, mango slush, long nights at the arcade, early mornings in bed. Please be same or similar.

@segasaga

Oklahoma City, OK

OPHTHALMOLOGIST ISO LOVE-SCAM ARTIST

27, anti-cuddling goofy bionic (from the waist down), seeking bi-polar (meaning your skin is black but you look white from the outside), bisexual (meaning you won't eat bison in bed)

If you are under 30, pansexual, butch, hard to love, think gardeners are deserts, vulnerable to bumblebees, bratty, and consistently passionate, you are not for me.

Everyone else, please persist or resist @alphaADHDfemme

PLAYTEST

Me: Furry, stuck in a hot tub, shop at Trader Joe's, licks a stick of salted chocolate, luv 2 steal from shops, a dog has chewn off my ankle and threatens my throat. The weather is turning. Be a hot water bottle for me.

You: Consummate shoplifter, sweet as peach cobbler, warm as a tiffin, shaped like mango, taste like whiskey.

@dreamme

Salt Lake City, Utah

BE MY BEEHIVE, BE MY BONER & CLYDE

I need someone sexy to blame
for all the great things
that are happening in my awesome life.
Or, you could be ugly & this is how it will roll: Do you want vacation
days or do you want my Sundays? Do you want happiness or do you want decor
What if I offer both?
I'm beautiful and I'm happy.
I need a soulmate who aren't either.
@hitmebabyhitthisdamnbabyrightaway

ALABAMA (where else?)

CUTE BOI LOOKING FOR A BOT

i am a cute, homosexual, polyglot, fashionista boi looking for my fairy femmebot. you must be 31+ with full frontal lobe fusion. External circuitry preferred. Let's stick forks into power outlets, climb a skyscraper with our slime, jump off the golden gate bridge into sweet narnia. cuddle me in my dreams; then let me cancel you.

@vroomvroom

Dublin, Ireland

FAT BUMBLEBEE IN SEARCH OF HER HONEY

You: great at giving hexagonal kisses, enjoy being stung, believe in the kind of love that existed sixty million years ago, into cross-pollination, cross-dressing

Me: antioxidant friendly, a sassy combo of black, gold, & positive rotundity, will devote my entire life (& force others too) to make you one teaspoon of honey, will fly a drone for you!

Pollen and sucrose lovers, come to my beehive! Allergic folks, leave your Kleenex box at the door.

@agrarianobesity
South Bend, IN (where all the boring people live)

LOOKING FOR MY PANADOL

curl up with me like a leaf. be my wellness dog. i'm always sick (but don't let that scare you!). who isn't sick in these days of anomie? indeed, if u are perennially well—i don't trust you. be sick with me, let's be sick machines.

@stickfiguresex
Seoul, South Korea

LET ME USE YOUR BODY TO WEAPONIZE LUST

& fetishize please & please & please
You are sugar & I am an oven.
You are baking sheet. I am flour.
You are liquid. I am brain.
You are fuck. I am bedsheet.
You are poetry. I am wind in which poetry climbs into.
You are luck & I am red envelope.

SO SO SO elope your word with my female anatomy.
@drinkmeuntilyouemptyallthegreatlakes

Milwaukee, WI

A LOVE AFFAIR FOR THE AGES

I believe in love. The old-fashioned kind: where I hide chocolates for you under library tables, send you tortured texts, stay up talking all night on the phone with you. Let's intersect in the worst of ways, the best of deaths. Let's be twisted together, burn in that sweet-sweet agony.

If you want a man for your dreams: that's me.
If you want a man to mow the lawn: that's me.
If you want a man to yell and scream at: that's me.
If you want a man to destroy: that's me.

@mucusandmuscles

Toronto, Canada

HUMAN COW IN SEARCH OF HER HUMAN WINDMILL

I have two pomelos that are oversized, aka too large. If I were to be pregnant, they would hold enough milk for the population of Southern California. Won't you be my natural breast reduction by spinning your four hands in circles in front of my moons?

Won't you be the kind of human turbine that compels my body to ebb and flow just by being near you? Won't you let me lap dance my huge breasts against your overdeveloped spine?

@idontbelieveinplasticsurgery

SIN CITY, NV

R U THE ONE FOR ME?

I should very much like to know.

Sister (not her real name) and I are seeking a third (you?) for our ménage à trois long overdue. We hope to triangulate obsolete forms of love; much akin to frolicking in the woods with the hungry bears and/or feeding ourselves to the overgrown snakes; you know, the kind of kink that knocks your fucking socks off. If this sounds like you—write to us with your super special peacock ink. @reelgoodsamaritan

Las Cruces, New Mexico

POLAR FEMME 4 SOLAR FEMME

Too hot to be a lesbian? Or too hypothermic?
Too high heeled to seal a kiss between thigh and polished nails?
Too hungry to eat a plate of linguini, eh, pussies? Love is arctic. Love is warm. Warm me up with the microwave of your mouth.
And, allow me to take the engine out of your solar panels.

@ecofriendlyfemme
Antarctica, Poland

LOOKING FOR MY HAPPY ENDING

Me: 30-something hardworking exec with a thirst for the adventurous and appreciation for the truly beautiful. I like scuba diving, surfing, and everything to do with the underwater world! Adore barbecue on the beach; just generally anything on the beach really.

You: Cute, adventurous, up for new things, have your shit together, and NOT boring! Let's explore each other's minds together and expand our worlds.

@papabear
Queens, NY

MYOPIC CINDERELLA 4 NON-BINARY CINDER

I scrub a lot because I work in the ER.
I am on my knees a lot because I love to please you.
I am dirty a lot from pressing my cinder face against you.
Send your mice-turned limousines and collect me at the border.
I return to my collective, ambient, post-doctorate soul after midnight.
You: my princess who doesn't believe in glass.
You: not afraid of happy ever after
You: look forward to my incision after a hard day of work.

You: @wonthavesexwithmystepsisters

Fargo, North Dakota

INUN-DATE ME WITH CHOCOLATE

I am the kind of person who likes to come home after another long, hard day at work to a partner who is just chockful of lovingkindness. That's it; that is all I want. Choke me with your dazzlingkindness. Stuff my mouth with loving ashes. Feed me bonemeal and the leftover scraps. Run me a bath of hot chocolate; toast me like marshmallow, burnt around the edges as my insides melt. After all this, when I'm reduced to quivering nothing—take me into your arms and tell me you love me, in your own special way.

Hmu. I know you're out there.
@ineedmorecoffee
Iowa City, Iowa

HELP ME TONGUE-CHOREOGRAPH OUR DESIRE

On a sheet of paper? Your bedsheets? Our dinning table?
Let you be my fork and I your wife.
Or you my spoon & I a reflection on your knife.
Me: nice, not bi, will cry, shy, won't say goodbye without dipping my fingers in dye,
always ask why, oh my.
You: a goon, will swoon & spoon with me under a full moon, fond of raccoons & sand dunes,
hate June, but will eat prunes,
willing to make love in the late afternoon,
willing to sing me a sexy tune before blowing me a balloon.
See you soon!

@yourfaithfulnapkinholder
Oslo, Norway

NEED A FURRY FOR THE WINTER

I'm looking for a raccoon-type lover
with human hands that can fit into genitals; scrape the bottom of my barrel;
a wily sense of food and where to find it; is always interested in eating,
always wants to eat me; will even steal me if need be; can creep around gardens at night,
looking like a burglar and feeling like a lover.

Be that raccoon for me. Steal my heart, clit, anus, and intestines.
Must be sexually dominant and unwilling to yield, not even an inch!

@bottomsup
Shreveport, Louisiana

SEEKING AN ABRASION-RESISTANT LOVER

For recreational and erotic usefulness. My sapphic view on love is quite simple: it has to be photovoltaic based, meaning, I am an extrovert, meaning I abduct solar energy from those (introverts, preferably) around me to rejuvenate. When we get together, I expect our sexual positions to fold, bend, be more portable than a folding Oru kayak. No electrical lovers in bed, please.

@yourlykanhypersport
Hialeah, Florida

A DATE FOR THE MOVIES

I just want a date for the movies.
Cue up for popcorn with me, hold hands in the seats, grope each other
in the darkness—pause for the good parts—and make out in the bathrooms after.
When the credits roll, we go home.
Me: 20-something, nerdy, love diet coke and ramen noodles.
You: 20-something with a taste for black leather.
Movie: Hong Kong action comedy only.

@asbestoshazard
Amherst, MA

BE MY TELESCOPIC CANCER SURVIVOR

Not related to astrology, but if you have cancer,
I have cancer too. Adenoacanthoma is mine. What is yours?
I hope yours is hematologically idyllic. My squamous cells could meet up with your blood cells
and we could break out in an endothelium dance. Seriously, life is too short and at
this stage (ignore the pun), no one wants to date us.
So let's make the most of it: let's create our own erotic clinical romantic
dinner: you eat my Italian plate of liver linguine & I eat your caper capellini.
Let's pussy eat ourselves towards death or cancer survival.
@lifeisshortbutmypastaisnt
Barcelona, Spain

NETFLIX AND CHILL

I would like a nontextual lover, one categorically opposed to all forms of sexts. That is: you must be corporeal, and deeply proud of your flesh and blood. Am particularly interested in trans-body love affairs i.e. give me your blood, replace my marrow with yours. My tongue sutured to your tongue. Your mind in mine.

NB: This is NOT a call for medical fetishists or similar thrill seekers. Only serious connoisseurs of cross-body love need apply.

@thegoldfinch
Lisbon, Portugal

TAKE ELEVATOR E TO THE PENTHOUSE OF MY HEART

& take elevator I to the anterior cul-de-sac of my vulva.
No matter which shaft you wish to take, I aim to please & then re-please.
The view from where I stand has no exit signs for feng shui or psychic malfunctioning.
Let me raise the bar of euphoria for your nervous systems.
Let me send a dolphin through Alibaba to your endorphins.
Architecturally speaking only, let me rebuild a coffin or two for all your heartaches.
Let me pull you into my arms while we wait for the moon to transform our love into a lake.

@houseofthetreeofgabbiani
Shenzhen, China

I WANNA KNOW WHAT LOVE IS

Me: a person without any hobbies, interests, or job prospects. I am not attractive. I eat too much and have chronic IBS. No friends, ever. Unskilled in masturbation and have never come. You: all of the above plus something more. You know. That special something. The super sauce. Fairy dust. Both of us, together: we break everything we touch, the men and women of the world shudder at our approach, we are mint with a hint of garlic on the breath.

@iknowyoucanshowme
Poughkeepsie, NY

INTERSECTIONAL SOFA LESBIANS ONLY!

I know it's a gift.
I know it's a kiss you can't easily dismiss.
Intersectional? You like to spread. Sofa? Certainly not a place to
huddle, definitely a place to cuddle. Lesbians? Obviously anything in high heels,
blouse with buttons that could heal, hear, & shield, long hair that
swings back and forth like a ancient torture whip, earrings that ring of lipstick & hip
& possibly infinity, curves that foreclose other curves, hipbones that speak of crater, constellation,
breakfast cereal bowls, & pillows. Only! It's safe to say: it's all about exclusion.
Possibly temptation. A sexy kind of limitation.

@lazboyswontdo
Fort Wayne, IN

LOOKING FOR MY FINAL GIRL

I want to creep around haunted houses with you, doing terrible things. I like grossness; viscera; the unseen regions of the body. We don't watch movies, we are the movie. You must be: busty, pure, virginal, just a touch sapphic. I am: youth greying into age, ripeness sliding into rot, black leather on red velvet, as scared of witches as I am in love.

Meet me where the night ends.

@chainsaw
Newt, TX

YOUR APPETIZER FOR MY DESSERT

I live on ice & don't believe in love at first sight. I also don't believe in unicorns or disruptive ruptures or futures. I'm just a Persian, demi-divergent, semi-daydreaming cat who won't just meow for milk or silk. I will certainly meow for sea debris & post-patriarchal carpooling of hands & tongues, that's if you are in the right lane. If your cunt is an extrovert and your heart an introvert, you are the perfect Nylon heartbeat for me!

@kissingonfirstdatesisintoverrated
Reykjavik, ICELAND

BE MY EXTREMITY

I have this fantasy.
You come as a friend; I keep you as a lover.
You want to leave; I nail you to the wall.
You want pasta; I eat your honeyed clit.
You want water; I pee on your face.
@fml
Lahore, Pakistan

INVASION IS A KIND OF PSYCHIC SEDATION

Sleeping & I are quiet lovers.
It's hard to notice us once we know who our foes are.
Are you my foes? Regardless, I need a third lover to get in between us:
between the streets and between our bedsheets. If you are pathetic then
I am nothing more than apathetic. If you are sad like an artichoke, I am that onion
that will make you cry harder. I know I know, you want to suck my toes and be my hoes.
Go ahead, I won't stop ya.

@yoursapphicnyquil

Buenos Aires, ARGENTINA

BE MY BOYRFRIEND

Be my bird, by me brain. Be my bee.

Me: young stud in need of love.
Pierced ears. Brazilian wax all over the place!
Looks are everything to me, and should be to you too.

You: an exotic, in search of adventure, incapable of giving head, badly in need of a blood transfusion (bite me like a bee-vampire; I'll give you all the blood in me!)

@sickinlove

Madison, WisconSIN

WEAR A DRESS & HELP THIS

Sensitive, bisexual clock find her second hand,
you know you know to make fisting more like an art instead of five finger
discounts at the deli-mart. Are you smart? Do you have any warts?
Have you been to Walmart?
Well. Well. What are you waiting for?
A pussy without a wig?
A U-haul without a driver?
A dyke without a bike?

@TimeToMowSomeBrazilianLawn

Rio de Janeiro, BRAZIL

A TOUCH OF SIN

Looking for a lipstick lesbian who can rock a red dress.
Let's make out in the strangest of places; in the backs of taxis; in fancy restaurants; in the sea. I'll lift your skirt and touch your clit, in public of course, in public; I'll let you be seen with me. Let you take selfies with me.
It'll all be real, and it won't ever end.
If interested, send a photo of you in your best dress to naughty_not_nice@hotmail.com
@naughtynice
Paris, France

AMNESIA INSIDE A SAPPHIC BREEZE?

Influence me
Make me fluent in women
Take me to a lip gloss coma
Help me file unemployment benefits for a comb.
Find my g-spot near Tom Hanks
Shrink my lymphnodes to a few numbers on a zipcode
Toss my mascara in a dyke bar
Dump my sport bras into a fish tank
Say what you will, but these are my clues for you to get into bed with me and my sex toys.

@vibratorsareforloudgirls
Columbus, Oh

TARZAN SEEKS JANE

or Jake

or another TARZAN

You must be feral, clean-shaved, and good with a sex swing. I have some toys I want to use and some more I want to invest in. I like anal punches and good hugs.

Neatfreaks need not apply.

@sauceontheside

Dallas, TX

QUEEN OF QUEER SUBLET

I have a small room, queen-size, in my roomy heart to sublet to anyone who is willing to pay a price for its profound coziness. The room is emotionally intelligent, has been through a lot, a romantic fire or two, eviction, etc. The room has so many windows: depart anytime or fly out whenever. Does not hold or take hostages erotically or emotionally. However, I take the following emolument:
Payment: won't take cash or venmo.
Payment: breakfast in bed, comedic sexts, some handful of deceased wild flowers.
Payment: dinner & a bug (any kind, dead preferably)
Payment: today (not tomorrow, tomorrow is too late)
Payment: you in one thong (preferably from Victoria's Secret)
@nopermanentloversplease
Amherst, MA

PEDANTIC BUT NOT PEDIATRIC

Me: Teacher (8th grade English), have the hots for all my students, looking for help in this department.

You: freshly graduated, scholarly but not a student, into age-play and/or teacher-student scenarios, willing to take the ruler sometimes—the caning of the bottom—the stuck-in-my-dungeon detention.

This is not a crime.
This is merely another sad exhibition.

@AnotherdayanotherA
Louiseville, KY

MY NEW YEAR RESOLUTIONS

I want: albino or blonde vegans, short boi, egg sandwiches, butch-friendly popcorn, Virgos, bisexuals, non-profit cats. What I don't want: lobster tails, flaming hot cheetos, high maintainance lesbians who know how to detassel corn, strong black umbrellas that can combat hurricanes or high wind

@indeedindeedindeed
Chesapeake, VA

WILL MOW YOUR LAWN FOR FREE

& other errands as required

Love is a transaction and I'm applying to a job. I'm applying to your opening. Take me in; adopt me. I promise to keep the place clean and the fire burning for when you return from your place of paid employment. I excel at oral sex, anal fun, soft massages of the whole body, risky modes of erotic excitation. Can cook Italian food exceedingly well.

Prefer soft butches, stone butches, or just plain butches, but am really open to anyone except a femme. That's my one hard limit (no femmes please). All else is on the table.
I know you're out there. Cum love this poor sweet baby <333

@lonelylonely
Fairbanks, AK

DYSLEXIC SEX TO REPLACE EXQUISITE LOVE

My heart is not a metal vase, incapable of breaking. My body isn't a temple, a place to worship or desecrate. I'm self-conscious, unsolid in a few private places. That being said, I don't expect to fall in love again. But I believe sex could replace uncertainty. A biological transaction that replaces memory, giving physical contact a new soundbite. You are a Mormon, not a moron. If you are a Mormon dyke, is having too many wives a bad thing? Just saying. You don't have to be beautiful, just good with your hands, and maybe your tongue. I sky-drive for a living.

@bemylesbianmemorystickformyvaginaharddrive
Salt Lake City, UT

I WANT TO FALL IN LOVE AGAIN

Hopeless romantic iso like-minded. All genders welcome. All body types. What's important is that we connect on a deep spiritual level (whatever spirituality means to you). I identify as a psychoslut, more potent than storm winds. Sexuality in all its forms is holy to me, and while I require sex at all times of the day I also adhere to certain rules and forms; nothing crazy, just respectful stuff. Buy me glass slippers; a room to fuck in; look at me like you'd do anything for me; then go ahead, do anything for me.

If you're a cool human with a respect for hedonism (even if you yourself aren't hedonist), we can be chill lol.

@thesandwichqueen

Mojave, CA

X-RAY MY NONBINARY BODY W/ WITH YOUR BINARY EYES

& hips & Southern tongue (Alabama, Georgia, etc—you must be born there if you want a fancy date w/ me). If you love eating chickens, oh man, oh man, & you're a Sagittarius baby, we should get married immediately. Should never wait. You can be fat, you can be intelligent, you can be curly like those curly fries, you can't, I repeat, can NOT, be a tree loving homo. Too much photosynthesis is like being high on weeds & you know I don't fucking love being high on weeds or seeds. & if you live w/ your mama, man oh man, do I find you so sexy!

Hook me up @yournuclearsunflower

Pyongyang, NORTH KOREA

PARTNER WANTED FOR ONE DATE

It's been raining all day where I am. It's romantic; the rain, cool wind, winter. I want to go for a long drive with the top down. We'd stop at a restaurant (your choice) and have a coffee and cheeseburger each. Then we watch a movie (my choice). We cuddle a little. On the way back, before I drop you home, we stop by a bar for a single drink each. You pay for my drink, I pay for yours. I drive you home. We never see each other again.

@hamster

Detroit, MI

JOVIAL ABOUT CASUAL STRANGULATION?

& high sex drive with an accent? But not French? Or European Anglo-saxophone? I have an abdominal appetite for swimming: my fingers the goldfish making their way towards your large body of water. I am soft and you are super-briny. We will lead a semi-decadent life: you in my white vegan arms while I read you poetry while serving you scallops * on a copper plate. Afterwards, I strangle you lightly without you knowing. But we agree that I let you swallow the nut-less truffle before I make you die a little. We all die a little inside from loving someone too much.

*(hey, I don't believe in forcing my fanatic politics on my lovers)

@chokingissexy

Omaha, NE

NOT ON THE REBOUND

I learned the word "rebound" in freshman year of college;
my roommate applied it to me. Since then I have been resisting the label.
You can help me here. I am: a young professional living in a major city, working
in pharamceuticals, in search of casual fun.

You can be anything, just anything, as long as you are: clean-shaved in
all the right places, hairy where it matters, an insatiable reader, kinky as fuck, super sincere.

I mean it: sincere.
I believe in sincerity and I hope you do too.
Let's plan our dates in advance, in spreadsheets, and carry them out to the T.

@notontherebound
Zzyzx, CA

52

KISS ME A MILLION TIMES ALREADY

I am that kind of girl. The one bathed in almond milk & honey. The one who isn't afraid of daffodils, lilacs, nor Uhaul in the middle of the road. The one who will kiss your neck even when the sun hasn't gone down on the moon. The one who hasn't had a bite to eat because she is too busy tasting the wine on your soft lips. The one who has a freshly kneaded dough in the oven because love is about having exposure to flame. Coffee in the late afternoon? Your arms wrap around me as I enter the door? You wearing a strap-on when I pull the oven door open?
@waterflourleavening
Nigeria

CHILL BOI ISO FWB

Let's be chill together. Smoke that kush and play video games. I wanna smash you against the screen; dip my fingers in yr pussy; then make you a cup of herbal tea and lose to you at Street Fighter. We can watch movies too. Take walks in the park. Make each other chill meals. Sleep over. I'll let you steal my clothes sometimes if you let me steal yours <3 Must be ready to meet irl, nice, kind, and—most importantly—CHILL
@likearicecube
Juneau, AK

ZERO TOLERANCE FOR ACADEMIC FEMME

Who won't have me. Zero! I clarify myself: zero! Me: sexy, verbose, high in fructose (hey, everyone has their weaknesses: mine, honeyed women in cool blazers who won't let me disrupt their ecosystem) odorless at times, gaudy, fun, have a low voice, astrological You: neurotic, academic femme (duh!), hoarse, drive a Subaru, self-conscious, magical, lazy (theoretically), casual (empirically), stubborn (only in bed)

@anallyfemme

Somewhere in Bolivia (can't let you know)

ISO NERDY SLUT

If you are supernerd, quirky, socially impeded (and abhor casual usage of term "social awkwardness"), collector of arcane knowledge, lover of the esoteric (though incapable of grasping the banal), and totally down to fuck -- hmu! I'm exactly who you think I am; between doses of coffee and ssri, I sink up out of the haze sometimes, supercharged with sexual magentism and that animal lust.

Come make me SUFFER.

@bottomlessabyss
San Francisco, CA

GOAT SHEPHERD ISO COOKIE WARMER FEMME OR CUTTER

I make one heck of a shepherd's pie, great at putting on makeup, and curling my eyelashes while tending my 23 goats. I am also good at milking (not just animals). Ready for 3.3 kids & artificial insemination (I don't expect us to have all the apparatus for this—help me crowdsource some sperm for us?). Each day, after I gather our goats into our byre, I like to stand & watch the sun fall asleep on the giant bosom of the earth. Like the sun, my life is simple, but I think my love for you is solar & enormous & possibly quite singular.

@onourfirstdateiofferyouafreshglassofgoatmilk
New Haven, CT

A DATE FOR THE NEW YEAR

My new year's resolution is to go on more dates. We can do this however you want it: you plan the dates or I do, you pay or I pay, we make out or we don't. I'm very open (as you can probably tell). I'm willing to travel, too, so distance is no barrier. I buy my own lube and equipment and am supercommunicative, so you'll never feel like you're being pressured into doing more than you want to.

I cook, am vegan (but you don't have to be), good with my hands (I garden for a living), and totally dig that fresh rain smell.

Looking for casual nsa fun—but if something more happens, I'm not one to say no.
@neversaynever
(wherever you need me to be)

EX-GENDERFLUID SUBARU WANTS A SONO SION W/ CONSERVATIVE BREASTS

Fast cars, fast lovers are overrated.
I like my women with bi-directional personality & noiseless (not voiceless) won't make
a sound during sex, eating out, or walking.
The slower you are the more I want you. I am slow & timeless
& don't want things to change too fast. I used to embrace everything
(genders, nouns, clowns), but with experience,
I realize that this philosophical stance is dangerous.
Forgive me if I want less of you, a safer version of you, a more
conservative edge of your Protestant climate.
Although unifocal, I can easily bifurcate you, like a tree after being chased by lightning.

Berlin, GERMANY

@yournearestcardealer

LOVE ME LIKE ICED COFFEE

Hey gurl. Come at me w/ a good coffee and I'll love you for the rest of my life.

Things I like to do: eat you out all day long, fuck your face off, fisting, pegging up the dirty laundry, rubbing your bruises, planting kisses all over your surface.

Things you like to do: eat me like pizza, slurp me like dairy.

We'll build log fires in the winter, swim in lakes in the summer. Looking for the missing piece? I will find you here, in printed things.

@licoriceandlace
Ho Chi Minh City, Vietnam

11:11 Press is an American independent literary publisher based in Minneapolis, MN. Founded in 2018, 11:11 publishes innovative literature of all forms and varieties. We believe in the right to freedom of artistic expression, the realization of creative potential, and the transcendental power of stories.